China's Economic Conditions

Wayne M. Morrison
Specialist in Asian Trade and Finance

June 26, 2012

Congressional Research Service

7-5700

www.crs.gov

RL33534

CRS Report for Congress ———————————
Prepared for Members and Committees of Congress

Summary

Prior to the initiation of economic reforms and trade liberalization 33 years ago, China maintained policies that kept the economy very poor, stagnant, centrally controlled, vastly inefficient, and relatively isolated from the global economy. Since opening up to foreign trade and investment and implementing free market reforms in 1979, China has been among the world's fastest growing economies, with real annual gross domestic product (GDP) averaging nearly 10% through 2011. In recent years, China has emerged as a major global economic and trade power. It is currently the world's second largest economy, largest merchandise exporter, second largest merchandise importer, second largest destination of foreign direct investment (FDI), largest manufacturer, largest holder of foreign exchange reserves, and largest creditor nation.

The global economic crisis that began in 2008 significantly affected China's economy. China's exports, imports, and FDI inflows declined, GDP growth slowed, and millions of Chinese workers reportedly lost their jobs. The Chinese government responded by implementing a $586 billion economic stimulus package, loosening monetary policies to increase bank lending, and providing various incentives to boost domestic consumption. Such policies enabled China to effectively weather the effects of the sharp global fall in demand for Chinese products, while several of the world's leading economies experienced negative or stagnant economic growth. From 2008 to 2011, China's real GDP growth averaged 9.6%.

Some economic forecasters project that China will overtake the United States as the world's largest economy within a few years, although U.S. per capita GDP levels are expected to remain much larger than that of China for many years to come. However, the ability of China to maintain a rapidly growing economy in the long run will depend largely on the ability of the Chinese government to implement comprehensive economic reforms that more quickly hasten China's transition to a free market economy; rebalance the Chinese economy by making consumer demand, rather than exporting and fixed investment, the main engine of economic growth; and boosting productivity and innovation. China faces numerous other challenges as well that could affect its future economic growth, such as widespread pollution, growing income disparities, an undeveloped social safety net, and extensive involvement of the state in the economy. The Chinese government has acknowledged that its current economic growth model needs to be altered. In October 2006, the Chinese government formally outlined a goal of building a "harmonious socialist society" by taking steps (by 2020) to lessen income inequality, improve the rule of law, enhance environmental protection, reduce corruption, and improve the country's social safety net (such as expanding health care and pension coverage to rural areas). In addition, the government announced plans to rebalance the economy and boost innovation.

China's economic rise has significant implications for the United States and hence is of major interest to Congress. On the one hand, China is a large (and potentially huge) export market for the United States. Many U.S. firms use China as the final point of assembly in their global supply chain networks. China's large holdings of U.S. Treasury securities help the federal government finance its budget deficits and keep U.S. interest rates low. However, some analysts contend that China maintains a number of distortive economic policies (such as an undervalued currency and protectionist industrial policies) that undermine U.S. economic interests. They warn that efforts by the Chinese government to promote innovation could mean that Chinese firms will increasingly pose a "competitive challenge" to many leading U.S. industries. This report surveys the rise of China's economy, describes major economic challenges facing China, and discusses the challenges, opportunities, and implications of China's economic rise for the United States.

Contents

Figures

Tables

Contacts

The rapid rise of China as a major economic power within a time span of about three decades is often described by analysts as one of the greatest economic success stories in modern times. From 1979 (when economic reforms began) to 2011, China's real gross domestic product (GDP) grew at an average annual rate of nearly 10%.[1] From 1980 to 2011, real GDP grew 19-fold in real terms, real per capita GDP increased 14-fold, and an estimated 500 million of people were raised out of extreme poverty. China is now the world's second largest economy and some analysts predict it could become the largest within a few years. Yet, on a per capita basis, China remains a relatively poor country.

China's economic rise has led to a substantial increase in U.S.-China economic ties. According to U.S. trade data, total trade between the two countries surged from $5 billion in 1980 to $503 billion in 2011. China is currently the United States' second largest trading partner, its third largest export market, and its largest source of imports. Many U.S. companies have extensive operations in China in order to sell their products in the booming Chinese market and to take advantage of lower-cost labor for export-oriented manufacturing.[2] These operations have helped some U.S. firms to remain internationally competitive and have supplied U.S. consumers with a variety of low-cost goods. China's large-scale purchases of U.S. Treasury securities (which totaled nearly $1.2 trillion at the end of 2011) have enabled the federal government to fund its budget deficits, which help keep U.S. interest rates relatively low.

However, the emergence of China as a major economic superpower has raised concern among many U.S. policymakers. Some claim that China uses unfair trade practices (such as an undervalued currency and subsidies given to domestic producers) to flood U.S. markets with low-cost goods, and that such practices threaten American jobs, wages, and living standards. Others contend that China's growing use of industrial policies to promote and protect certain domestic Chinese industries firms favored by the government, and its failure to take effective action against widespread infringement of U.S. intellectual property rights (IPR) in China, threaten to undermine the competitiveness of U.S. IP-intensive industries. In addition, while China has become a large and growing market for U.S. exports, critics contend that numerous trade and investment barriers limit opportunities for U.S. firms to sell in China, or force them to set up production facilities in China as the price of doing business there. Other concerns relating to China's economic growth include its growing demand for energy and raw materials and its emergence as the world's largest emitter of greenhouse gasses.

The Chinese government views a growing economy as vital to maintaining social stability. However, China faces a number of major economic challenges which could undermine future growth, including distortive economic policies that have resulted in over-reliance on fixed investment and exports for economic growth (rather than on consumer demand), government support for state-owned firms, a weak banking system, widening income gaps, growing pollution, and the relative lack of the rule of law in China. Many economists warn that such problems could undermine China's future economic growth. The Chinese government has acknowledged these problems and has pledged to address them by implementing policies to boost consumer spending, expand social safety net coverage, and encourage the development of less-polluting industries.

---

[1] The beginning of China's economic reform process began in December 1978 when the Third Plenum of the Eleventh Central Committee of the Communist Party adopted Deng Xiaoping's economic proposals. Implementation of the reforms began in 1979.

[2] Some companies use China as part of their global supply chain for manufactured parts, which are then exported and assembled elsewhere. Other firms have shifted the production of finished products from other countries (mainly in Asia) to China; they import parts and materials into China for final assembly.

This report provides background on China's economic rise, describes its current economic structure, identifies the challenges China faces to keep its economy growing strong, and discusses the challenges, opportunities, and implications of China's economic rise for the United States.

The History of China's Economic Development

China's Economy Prior to Reforms

Prior to 1979, China, under the leadership of Chairman Mao Zedong, maintained a centrally planned, or command, economy. A large share of the country's economic output was directed and controlled by the state, which set production goals, controlled prices, and allocated resources throughout most of the economy. During the 1950s, all of China's individual household farms were collectivized into large communes. To support rapid industrialization, the central government undertook large-scale investments in physical and human capital during the 1960s and 1970s. As a result, by 1978 nearly three-fourths of industrial production was produced by centrally controlled, state-owned enterprises (SOEs), according to centrally planned output targets. Private enterprises and foreign-invested firms were generally barred. A central goal of the Chinese government was to make China's economy relatively self-sufficient. Foreign trade was generally limited to obtaining only those goods that could not be made or obtained in China.

Government policies kept the Chinese economy relatively stagnant and inefficient, mainly because most aspects of the economy were managed and run by the central government (and thus there were few profit incentives for firms, workers, and farmers), competition was virtually nonexistent, foreign trade and investment flows were mainly limited to Soviet bloc countries, and price and production controls caused widespread distortions in the economy. Chinese living standards were substantially lower than those of many other developing countries. The Chinese government in 1978 (shortly after the death of Chairman Mao in 1976) decided to break with its Soviet-style economic policies by gradually reforming the economy according to free market principles and opening up trade and investment with the West, in the hope that this would significantly increase economic growth and raise living standards. As Chinese leader Deng Xiaoping, the architect of China's economic reforms, put it: "Black cat, white cat, what does it matter what color the cat is as long as it catches mice?"[3]

The Introduction of Economic Reforms

Beginning in 1979, China launched several economic reforms. The central government initiated price and ownership incentives for farmers, which enabled them to sell a portion of their crops on the free market. In addition, the government established four special economic zones along the coast for the purpose of attracting foreign investment, boosting exports, and importing high technology products into China. Additional reforms, which followed in stages, sought to decentralize economic policymaking in several sectors, especially trade. Economic control of various enterprises was given to provincial and local governments, which were generally allowed to operate and compete on free market principles, rather than under the direction and guidance of

---

[3] This reference appears to have meant that it did not matter whether an economic policy was considered to be capitalist or socialist, what really mattered was whether that policy boosted the economy.

state planning. In addition, citizens were encouraged to start their own businesses. Additional coastal regions and cities were designated as open cities and development zones, which allowed them to experiment with free market reforms and to offer tax and trade incentives to attract foreign investment. In addition, state price controls on a wide range of products were gradually eliminated. Trade liberalization was also a major key to China's economic success. Removing trade barriers encouraged greater competition and attracted foreign direct investment (FDI) inflows.[4] China's gradual implementation of economic reforms sought to identify which policies produced favorable economic outcomes (and which did not) so that they could be implemented in other parts of the country, a process Deng Xiaoping reportedly referred to as "crossing the river by touching the stones."[5]

China's Economic Growth Since Reforms: 1979-2012

Since the introduction of economic reforms, China's economy has grown substantially faster than during the pre-reform period (see **Table 1**). According to the Chinese government, from 1953 to 1978, real annual GDP growth was estimated at 6.7%,[6] although many analysts claim that Chinese economic data during this period are highly questionable because government officials often exaggerated production levels for a variety of political reasons.[7] Agnus Maddison estimates China's average annual real GDP during this period at 4.4%.[8]

China's economy suffered economic downturns during the leadership of Chairman Mao Zedong, including during the Great Leap Forward from 1958-1960 (which led to a massive famine and reportedly the death of tens of millions of people) and the Cultural Revolution from 1966-1976 (which caused political chaos and greatly disrupted the economy). During the reform period (1979-2011), China's average annual real GDP grew by 9.9%. This essentially has meant that, on average China has been able to double the size of its economy in real terms every eight years.

The global economic slowdown, which began in 2008, impacted the Chinese economy (especially the export sector). China's real GDP growth fell from 14.2% in 2007 to 9.6% in 2008 to 9.2% in 2009. In response, the Chinese government implemented a large economic stimulus package and an expansive monetary policy. These measures boosted domestic investment and consumption and helped prevent a sharp economic slowdown in China. In 2010, China's real GDP grew by 10.4%, and in 2011 it rose by 9.2%. During the first quarter of 2012, real GDP growth was 8.1% on a year-on-year basis.

---

[4] For example, China's accession to the World Trade Organization in December 2001, which required it to reduce a wide range of trade and investment barriers, helped to accelerate GDP growth and led to a sharp increase in FDI flows to China.

[5] Many analysts contend that Deng's push to implement economic reforms was largely motivated by a belief that the resulting economic growth would ensure that the Communist Party stayed in power.

[6] Chinability, *GDP Growth in China, 1952-2011*, at http://www.chinability.com/GDP htm.

[7] During the Great Leap Forward, local Chinese officials are believed to have often exaggerated agricultural production to prove their ability to implement Mao's economic policies in order to advance their careers or to avoid getting into political trouble with Beijing. Central government officials may have also exaggerated China's economic statistics in order to illustrate the "success" of the government's economic policies.

[8] The Organization for Economic Cooperation and Development, *Chinese Economic Performance in the Long Run, 960-2030*, by Angus Maddison, 2007.

Table 1. China's Average Annual Real GDP Growth: 1979-2012

Year	Real Growth Rate (%)
1979	7.6
1980	7.9
1981	5.3
1982	9.0
1983	10.9
1984	15.2
1985	13.5
1986	8.9
1987	11.6
1988	11.3
1989	4.1
1990	3.8
1991	9.2
1992	14.2
1993	13.9
1994	13.1
1995	10.9
1996	10.0
1997	9.3
1998	7.8
1999	7.6
2000	8.4
2001	8.3
2002	9.1
2003	10.0
2004	10.1
2005	11.3
2006	12.7
2007	14.2
2008	9.6
2009	9.2
2010	10.4
2011	9.2
2012 First Quarter	8.1

Source: Economist Intelligence Unit, based on official Chinese government data.

Note: Data for 2012 are year-on-year.

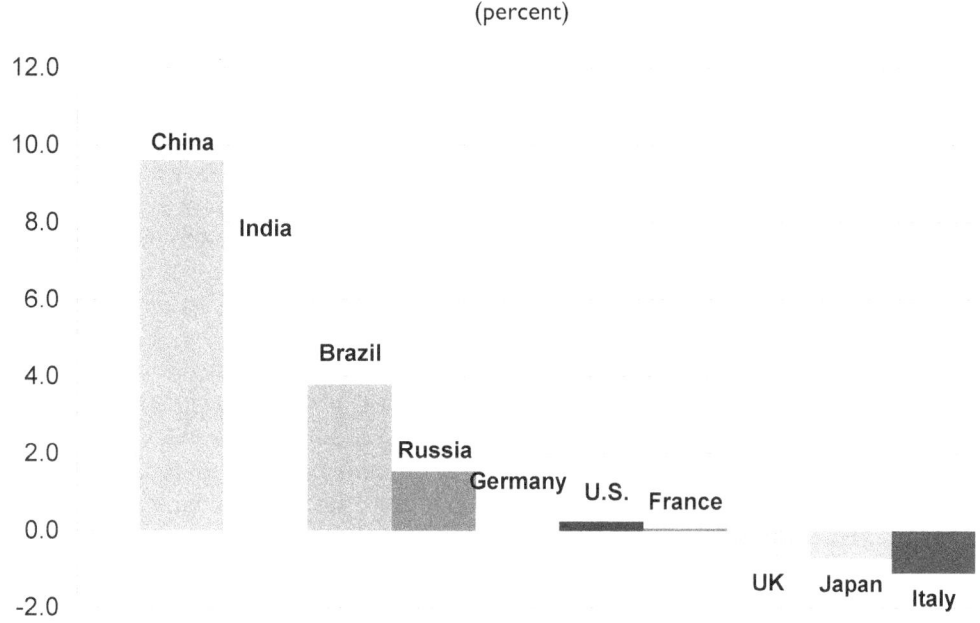

Figure 1. Average Real GDP Growth Among Major Global Economies: 2008-2011

(percent)

Source: EIU database.

Causes of China's Economic Growth

Economists generally attribute much of China's rapid economic growth to two main factors: large-scale capital investment (financed by large domestic savings and foreign investment) and rapid productivity growth. These two factors appear to have gone together hand in hand. Economic reforms led to higher efficiency in the economy, which boosted output and increased resources for additional investment in the economy.

China has historically maintained a high rate of savings. When reforms were initiated in 1979, domestic savings as a percentage of GDP stood at 32%. However, most Chinese savings during this period were generated by the profits of SOEs, which were used by the central government for domestic investment. Economic reforms, which included the decentralization of economic production, led to substantial growth in Chinese household savings as well as corporate savings. As a result, China's gross savings as a percentage of GDP has steadily risen, reaching 53.9% in 2010 (compared to a U.S. rate of 9.3%), and is among the highest savings rates in the world.[9] The large level of savings has enabled China to boost domestic investment. In fact, its gross domestic savings levels far exceed its domestic investment levels, meaning that China is a large net global lender.

Several economists have concluded that productivity gains (i.e., increases in efficiency) have been another major factor in China's rapid economic growth. The improvements to productivity were caused largely by a reallocation of resources to more productive uses, especially in sectors that were formerly heavily controlled by the central government, such as agriculture, trade, and

---

[9] Source: Economist Intelligence Unit Database.

services. For example, agricultural reforms boosted production, freeing workers to pursue employment in the more productive manufacturing sector. China's decentralization of the economy led to the rise of non-state enterprises (such as private firms), which tended to pursue more productive activities than the centrally controlled SOEs and were more market-oriented, and hence, more efficient. Additionally, a greater share of the economy (mainly the export sector) was exposed to competitive forces. Local and provincial governments were allowed to establish and operate various enterprises on market principles, without interference from the central government. In addition, FDI in China brought with it new technology and processes that boosted efficiency. As indicated in **Figure 2**, China has achieved high rates of total factor productivity (TFP) growth relative to the United States. TFP represents an estimate of the part of economic output growth not accounted for by the growth in inputs (such as labor and capital), and is often attributed to the effects of technological change and efficiency gains. China experiences faster TFP growth than most developed countries such as the United States because of its ability to access and utilize existing foreign technology and know-how. High TFP growth rates have been a major factor behind China's rapid economic growth rate. However, as China's technological development begins to approach that of major developed countries, its level of productivity gains, and thus, real GDP growth, could slow significantly from its historic 10% average, unless China becomes a major center for new technology and innovation and/or implements new comprehensive economic reforms.[10] As indicated in **Figure 3**, the EIU currently projects that China's real GDP growth will slow considerably in the years ahead, averaging 7.0% from 2012 to 2020, and falling to 3.7% from 2021 to 2030.[11]

The Chinese government has indicated its desire to move away from its current economic model of fast growth at any cost to more "smart" economic growth, which seeks to reduce reliance on energy-intensive and high-polluting industries and rely more on high technology, green energy, and services. China also has indicated it wants to obtain more balanced economic growth. (These issues are discussed in more detail later in the report.)

---

[10] Like China, Japan experienced rapid economic growth during the early stages of its development in the post-WWII era, with real GDP averaging 11.0% from 1960-1970. However, from 1970-1980 real GDP averaged 5.4%; it was 4.1% from 1980-1990, 1.1% from 1990-2000. Japan has continued to experience relatively stagnant economic growth, in part because of its inability to address a number of structural economic problems. See CRS Report RL30176, *Japan's "Economic Miracle": What Happened?*, by William H. Cooper

[11] Note, long-term economic projections should be viewed with caution.

Figure 2. Comparison of Annual Changes in Total Factor Productivity in China and the United States: 2000-2011

(percent)

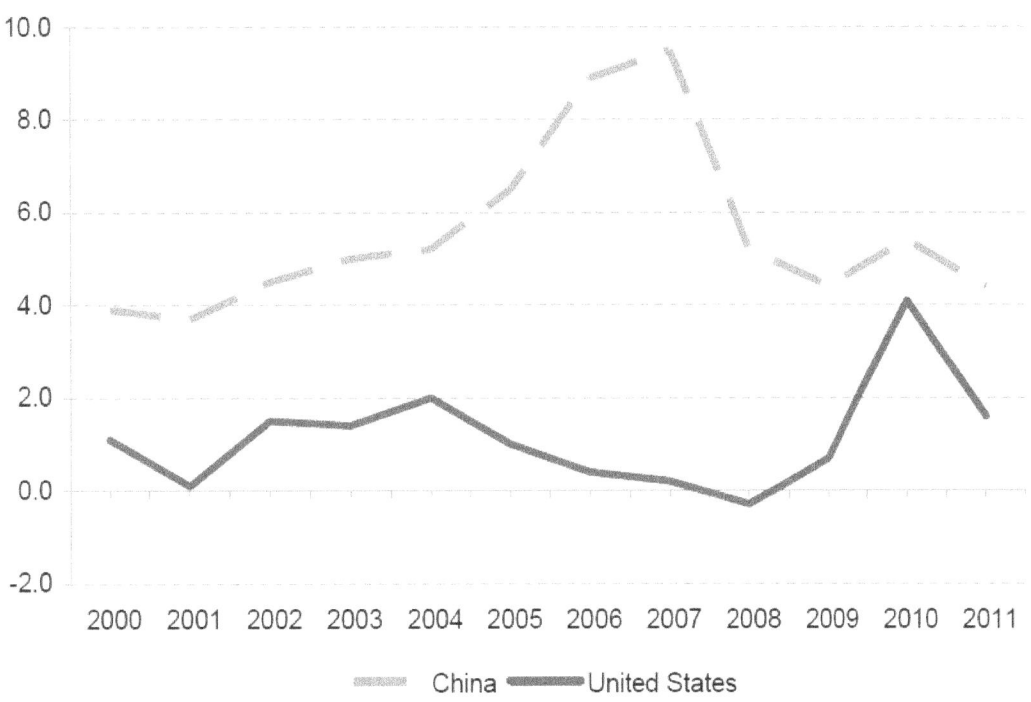

Source: Estimated by the Economist Intelligence Unit.

Note: Total factor productivity represents the part of economic output growth not accounted for by the growth in inputs, such as labor and capital, and is often used to estimate the effects of technological change.

Figure 3. Projections of U.S. and Chinese Annual Real GDP Growth: 2012-2030

%

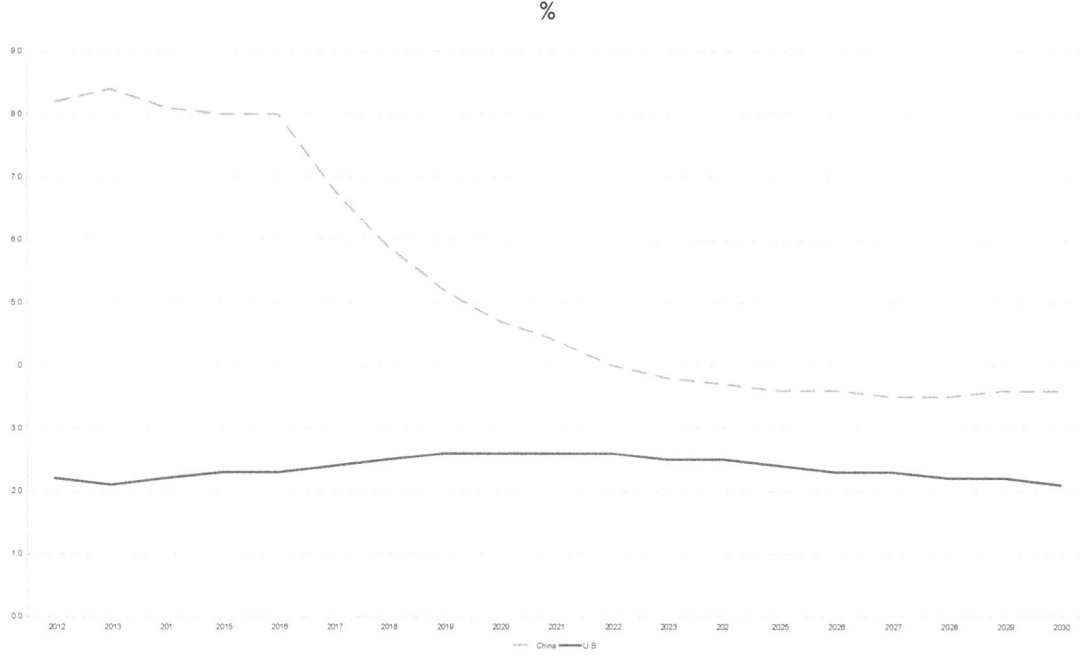

Source: Economist Intelligence Unit.

Note: Long-term economic projections should be interpreted with caution

Measuring the Size of China's Economy

The rapid growth of the Chinese economy has led many analysts to speculate if and when China will overtake the United States as the "world's largest economic power." The "actual" size of China's economy has been a subject of extensive debate among economists. Measured in U.S. dollars using nominal exchange rates, China's GDP in 2011 was $7.2 trillion, less than half the size of the U.S. economy.[12] The per capita GDP (a common measurement of a country's living standards) of China was $5,460, which was 12% the size of Japan's level and 11% that of the United States (see **Table 2**).

Many economists contend that using nominal exchange rates to convert Chinese data (or that of other countries) into U.S. dollars fails to reflect the true size of China's economy and living standards relative to the United States. Nominal exchange rates simply reflect the prices of foreign currencies vis-à-vis the U.S. dollar and such measurements exclude differences in the prices for goods and services across countries. To illustrate, one U.S. dollar exchanged for local currency in China would buy more goods and services there than it would in the United States. This is because prices for goods and services in China are generally lower than they are in the United States. Conversely, prices for goods and services in Japan are generally higher than they are in the United States (and China). Thus, one dollar exchanged for local Japanese currency would buy fewer goods and services there than it would in the United States. Economists attempt

---

[12] On a nominal dollar basis, China overtook Japan in 2010 to become the world's second largest economy (after the United States).

to develop estimates of exchange rates based on their actual purchasing power relative to the dollar in order to make more accurate comparisons of economic data across countries, usually referred to as a purchasing power parity (PPP) basis.

The PPP exchange rate increases the (estimated) measurement of China's economy and its per capita GDP. According the Economist Intelligence Unit, (EIU), which utilizes World Bank data, prices for goods and services in China are 41.5% the level they are in the United States. Adjusting for this price differential raises the value of China's 2011 GDP from $7.2 trillion (nominal dollars) to $11.4 trillion (on a PPP basis).[13] This would indicate that China's economy is 76.0% the size of the U.S. economy. China's share of global GDP on a PPP basis rose from 3.7% in 1990 to 14.3% in 2011 (the U.S. share of global GDP peaked at 24.3% in 1999 and declined to 18.9% in 2011), see **Figure 4**.

Many economic analysts predict that a PPP basis China will soon overtake the United States as the world's largest economy. EIU, for example, projects this will occur by 2016, and that by 2030, China's economy could be 30% larger than that of the United States.[14] This would not be the first time in history that China was the world's largest economy (see text box).

The Decline and Rise of China's Economy

According to a study by economist Angus Maddison, China was the world's largest economy in 1820, accounting for an estimated 32.9% of global GDP. However, foreign and civil wars, internal strife, weak and ineffective governments, natural disasters (some of which were man-made) and distortive economic policies caused China's share of global GDP on a PPP basis to shrink significantly. By 1952, China's share of global GDP had fallen to 5.2%, and by1978, it slid to 4.9%.[15] The adoption of economic reforms by China in the late 1970s led to a surge in China's economic growth and has help restore China as major a global economic power.

Source: The Organization for Economic Cooperation and Development, *Chinese Economic Performance in the Long Run, 960-2030*, by Angus Maddison, 2007.

The PPP measurement also raises China's 2011 per capita GDP (from $5,460) to $8,650, which was 17.9% of the U.S. level. The EIU projects this level will rise to 34.3% by 2030. Thus, although China will likely become the world's largest economy in a few years on a PPP basis, it will likely take many years for its living standards to approach U.S. levels.[16]

---

[13] In other words, the PPP data reflect what the value of China's goods and services would be if they were sold in the United States.

[14] However, such long-term economic projections should be viewed with caution.

[15] In comparison, the U.S. share of global GDP rose from 1.8% in 1820 to 27.5% in 1952, but declined to 21.6% by 1978.

[16] EIU database, surveyed on May 22, 2012.

Table 2. Comparisons of Chinese, Japanese, and U.S. GDP and Per Capita GDP in Nominal U.S. Dollars and a Purchasing Power Parity Basis: 2011

	China	Japan	United States
Nominal GDP ($ billions)	7,208	5,871	15,094
GDP in PPP ($ billions)	11,425	4,384	15,094
Nominal Per Capita GDP ($)	5,460	46,420	48,410
Per Capita GDP in PPP ($)	8,650	34,660	48,410

Source: Economist Intelligence Unit estimates using World Bank PPP data.

Figure 4. Chinese and U.S. GDP as a Percent of Global Total: 1990-2011 and Projections through 2016

(percent)

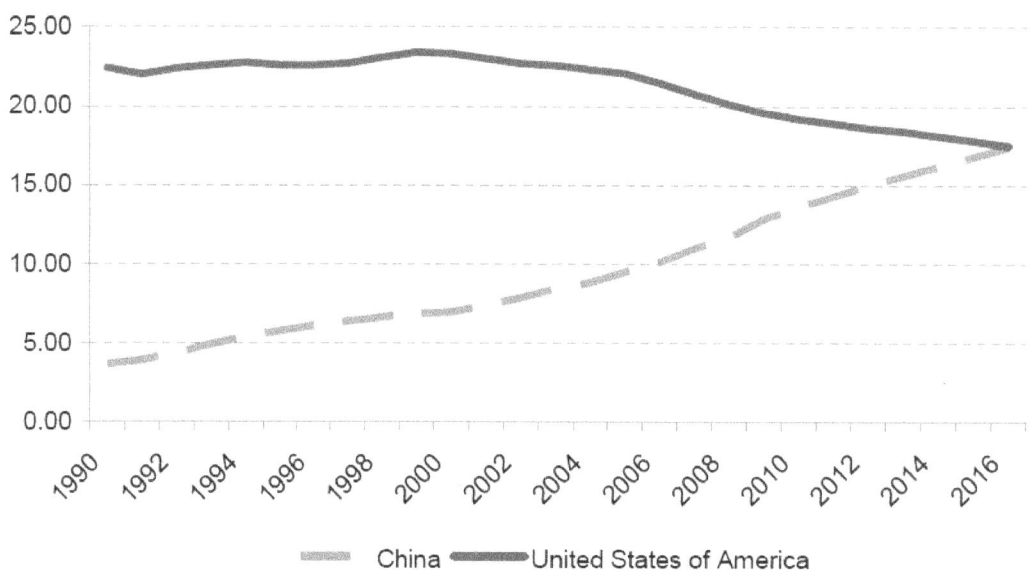

Source: Economist Intelligence Unit

Note: Based on estimates of GDP on a PPP basis.

Foreign Direct Investment (FDI) in China

China's trade and investment reforms and incentives led to a surge in FDI beginning in the early 1990s. Such flows have been a major source of China's productivity gains and rapid economic and trade growth. There were reportedly 445,244 foreign-invested enterprises (FIEs) registered in China in 2010, employing 55.2 million workers or 15.9% of the urban workforce.[17] As indicated in **Figure 5**, FIEs account for a significant share of China's industrial output. That level rose from

---

[17] China 2011 Statistical Yearbook.

2.3% in 1990 to a high of 35.9% in 2003, but fell to 27.1% by 2010.[18] In addition, FIE's are responsible for a significant level of China's foreign trade. In 2011, FIEs in China accounted for 52.4% of China's exports and 49.6% of its imports, although this level was down from its peak in 2006 when FIEs' share of Chinese exports and imports was 58.2% and 59.7%, respectively, as indicated in **Figure 6**. FIEs in China dominate China's high technology exports. From 2002 to 2010, the share of China's high tech exports by FIEs rose from 79% to 82%. During the same period, the share of China's high tech exports by wholly owned foreign firms (which excludes foreign joint ventures with Chinese firms), rose from 55% to 67%.

Figure 5. Industrial Output by Foreign-Invested Firms in China as a Share of National Total: 1990-2010

(percent)

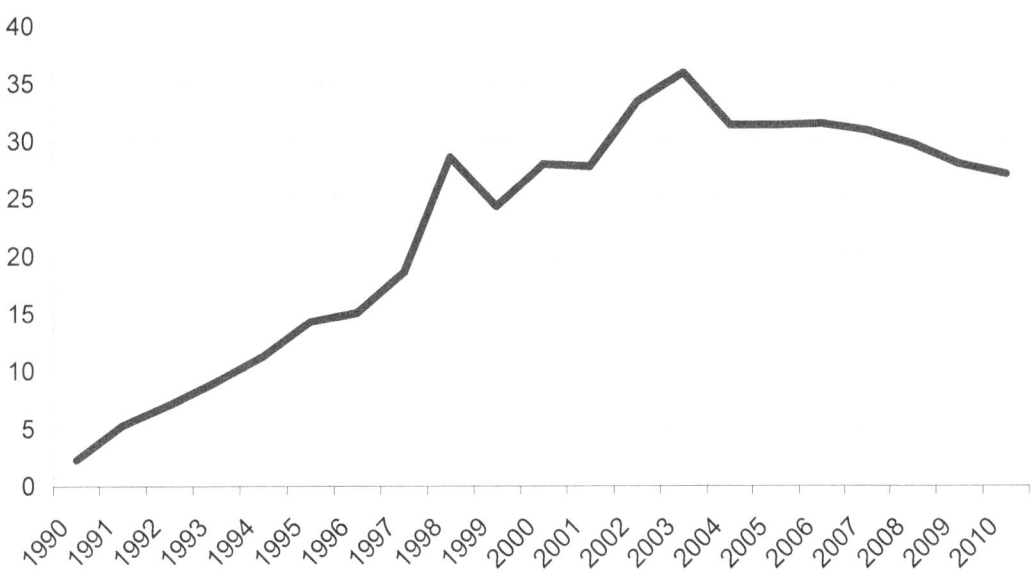

Source: Invest in China (www.fdi.gov.cn)

---

[18] Industrial output is defined by the Chinese government as the total volume of final industrial products produced and industrial services provided during a given period. Source: China 2011 Statistical Yearbook.

Figure 6. Share of China's Exports and Imports Attributed to Foreign-Invested Enterprises in China: 1990-2012*

(percent)

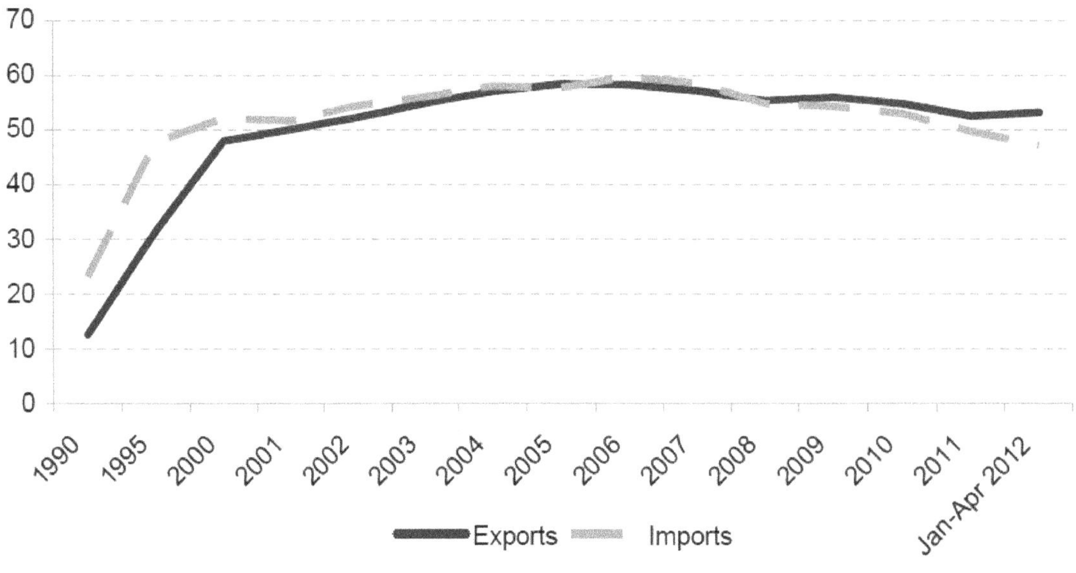

Source: "Invest in China (http://www.fdi.gov.cn/pub/FDI_EN/default.htm)

Note: Data for 2012 are January-April 2012.

According to the Chinese government, annual FDI inflows into China grew from $2 billion in 1985 to $108 billion in 2008. Due to the effects of the global economic slowdown, FDI flows to China fell by 12.2% to $90 billion in 2009. They totaled $106 billion in 2010 and $116 billion in 2011 (see **Figure 7**). Chinese data for January-May 2012 indicate that FDI fell by 1.9% on a year-on-year basis. Hong Kong was reported as the largest source of FDI flows to China in 2011 (63.9% of total), followed by Taiwan, Japan, and Singapore, and the United States. Accoording to Chinese data, annual U.S. FDI flows to China peaked at $5.4 billion in 2002 (10.2% of total FDI in China). In 2011, they were $3.0 billion or 2.6% of total (see **Figure 9**).[19]

The cumulative level (or stock) of FDI in China at the end of 2011 is estimated at $1.2 trillion, making it one of the world's largest destinations of FDI. According to the United Nations Conference on Trade and Development, China was the world's second largest destination for FDI flows in 2011, after the United States (see **Figure 8**). The largest sources of cumulative FDI in China for 1979-2011 were Hong Kong (43.5% of total), the British Virgin Islands, Japan, the United States, and Taiwan (see **Table 3**).[20]

---

[19] U.S. data on bilateral FDI flows with China differ significantly with Chinese data. For additional info on bilateral FDI flows based on U.S. data, see CRS Report RL33536, *China-U.S. Trade Issues*, by Wayne M. Morrison.

[20] Much of the FDI originating from the British Virgin Islands and Hong Kong may originate from other foreign investors. In addition, some Chinese investors might be using these locations to shift funds overseas in order to re-invest in China to take advantage of preferential investment policies (this practice is often referred to as "round-tipping"). Thus, the actual level of FDI in China may be overstated.

Figure 7. Annual FDI Flows to China: 1985-2011

($ billions)

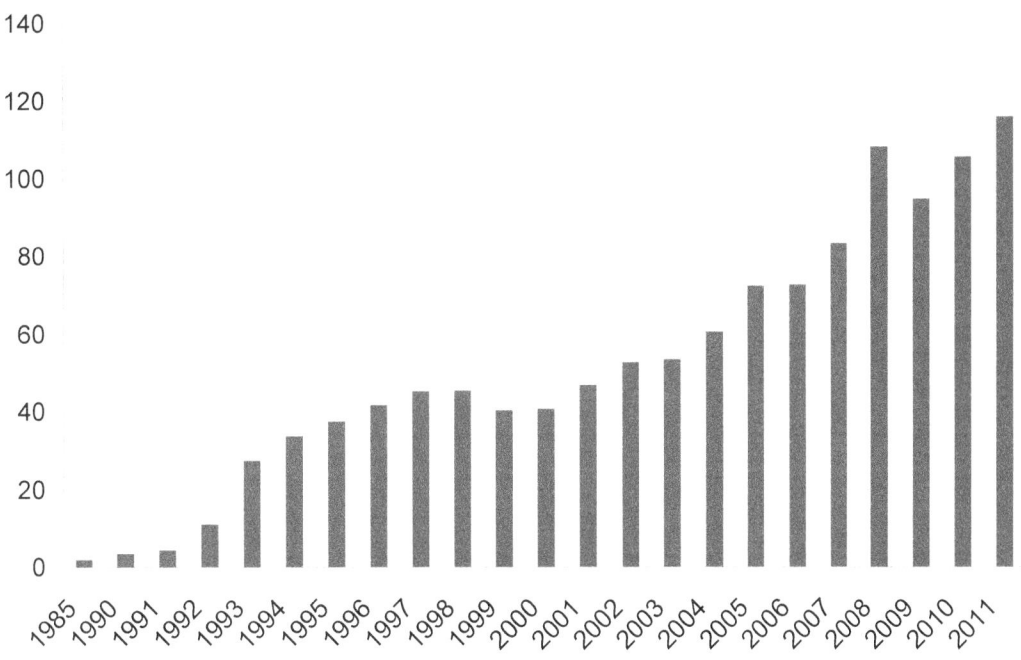

Source: United Nations Conference on Trade and Investment and Invest China.

Figure 8. Major Recipients of Global FDI Inflows in 2011

($ billions)

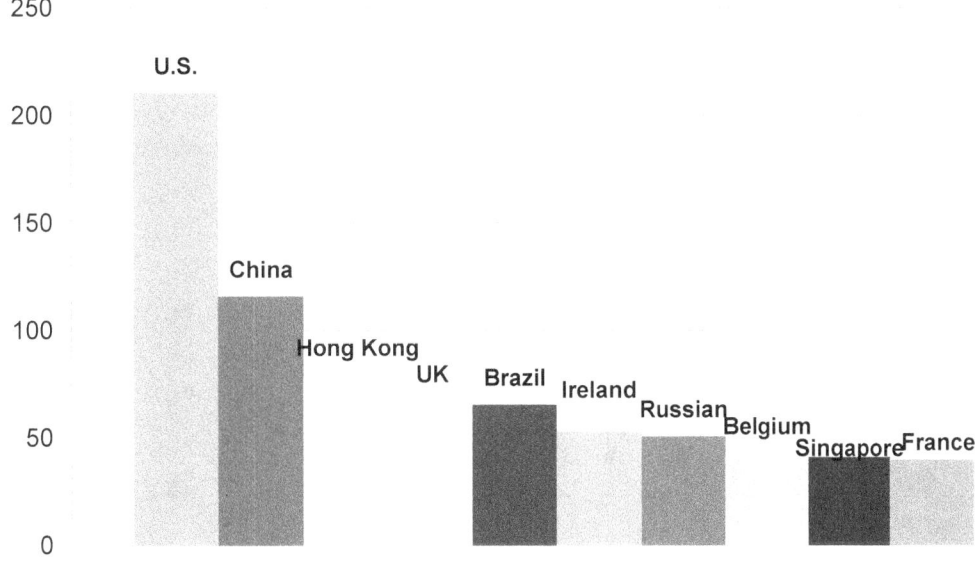

Source: United Nations Conference on Trade and Investment and Invest and Chinese Ministry of Commerce

Note: Data for China are official Chinese data; all are estimates by the United Nations.

Table 3. Major Sources of FDI in China: 1979-2011

($ billions and % of total)

Country	Estimated Cumulative Utilized FDI: 1979-2011		Utilized FDI in 2011	
	Amount	% of Total	Amount	% of Total
Total	1,224.0	100.0	116.1	100.0
Hong Kong	533.2	43.5	77.0	66.3
British Virgin Islands*	111.8	9.1	NA	NA
Japan	79.9	6.5	6.3	5.4
United States	68.1	5.6	3.0	2.6
Taiwan	58.7	4.8	6.7	5.8
Singapore	53.4	4.5	6.3	5.4
South Korea	49.9	4.1	2.6	2.2

Source: Chinese Ministry of Commerce and Chinese Statistical Yearbook.

Notes: Ranked by cumulative top seven sources of FDI in China through 2011. *Data for the British Virgin Islands are through 2010.

Figure 9. Annual U.S. FDI Flows to China: 1985-2011

($ millions)

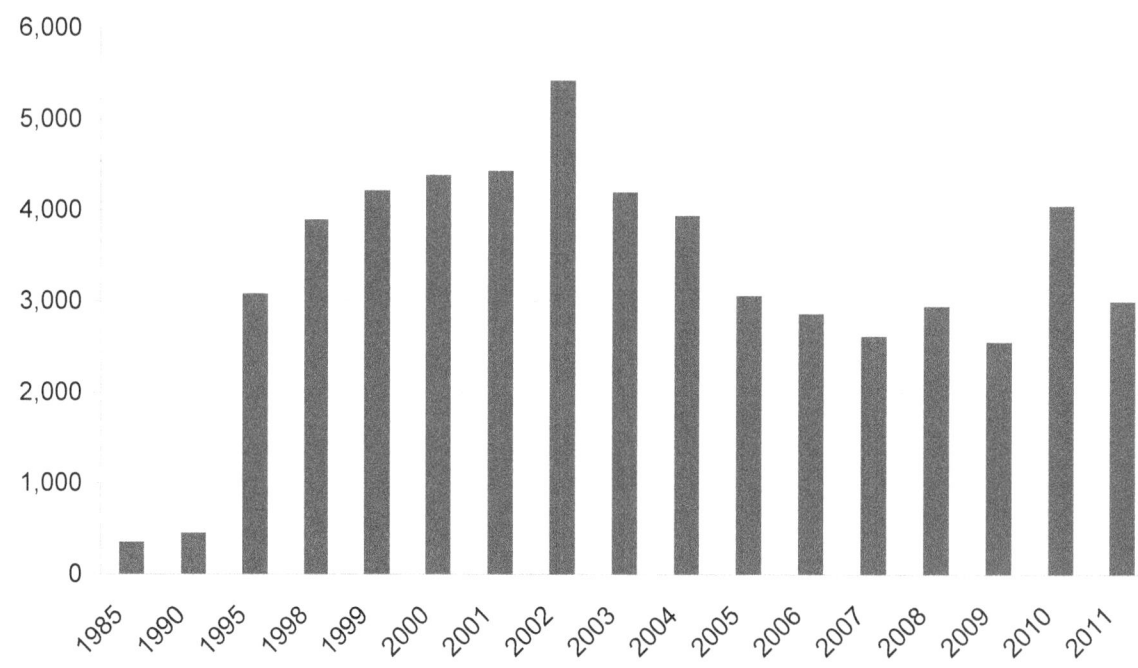

Source: Chinese Ministry of Commerce and Chinese Yearbook, various years.

Note: Chinese and U.S. data on bilateral FDI flows differ sharply because of different methodologies used.

China's Growing FDI Outflows

A key aspect of China's economic modernization and growth strategy during the 1980s and 1990s was to attract FDI into China to help boost the development of domestic firms. Investment by Chinese firms abroad was sharply restricted. However, in 2000, China's leaders initiated a new "go global" strategy, which sought to encourage Chinese firms (primarily SOEs) to invest overseas. One key factor driving this investment is China's massive accumulation of foreign exchange reserves, Traditionally much of those reserves have been invested in relatively safe, but low-yielding, assets, such as U.S. Treasury securities. On September 29, 2007, the Chinese government officially launched the China Investment Corporation (CIC) in an effort to seek more profitable returns on its foreign exchange reserves and diversify away from its U.S. dollar holdings. The CIC was originally funded at $200 billion, making it one of the world's largest sovereign wealth funds.[21] Another factor behind the government's drive to encourage more outward FDI flows has been to obtain natural resources, such as oil and minerals, deemed by the government as necessary to sustain China's rapid economic growth.[22] In June 2005, the China National Offshore Oil Corporation (CNOOC), through its Hong Kong subsidiary (CNOOC Ltd.), made a bid to buy a U.S. energy company, UNOCAL, for $18.5 billion, although CNOOC later withdrew its bid due to opposition by several congressional Members. Finally, the Chinese government has indicated its goal of developing globally competitive Chinese firms with their own brands. Investing in foreign firms, or acquiring them, is viewed as a method for Chinese firms to obtain technology, management skills, and often, internationally recognized brands, needed to help Chinese firms become more globally competitive. For example, in April 2005 Lenovo Group Limited, a Chinese computer company, purchased IBM Corporation's personal computer division for $1.75 billion.[23] Similarly, overseas FDI in new plants and businesses is viewed as developing multinational Chinese firms with production facilities and R&D operations around the world.

China has become a significant source of global FDI outflows, which rose from $2.7 billion in 2002 to $67.6 billion in 2011 (see **Figure 10**). In 2011, China ranked as the 9th largest source of global FDI, according to the United Nations (see **Figure 11**).[24] The stock of China's outward FDI through 2011 is estimated at $384.9 billion.

China's data indicate that the top five destinations of its FDI outflows in 2010 were Hong Kong (which accounted for 56.5% of total), the British Virgin Islands, the Cayman Islands, Luxembourg, and Australia (the United States ranked 7th). In terms of the stock of Chinese FDI outflows, the largest destinations were Hong Kong (62.8% of total), the British Virgin Islands, the Cayman Islands, Australia, and Singapore (the United States ranked 7th).[25] According to China's Ministry of Commerce, four out of 10 of biggest overseas Chinese corporate investors were oil companies (based on FDI stock through 2010).[26]

---

[21] See, CRS Report RL34337, *China's Sovereign Wealth Fund*, by Michael F. Martin.

[22] Chinese oil and mineral companies are dominated by SOEs.

[23] The Chinese government is believed to be Lenovo's largest shareholder.

[24] United Nations Conference on Trade and Development, Global Investment Trade Monitor, April 12, 2012.

[25] It is likely that a significant level of Chinese FDI in the British Virgin Islands, the Cayman Islands, and Hong Kong are re-directed elsewhere.

[26] Chinese Ministry of Commerce, *2010 Statistical Bulletin of China's Outward Foreign Direct Investment*, October 2011.

According to A Capital Dragon Index, a firm that tracks China's FDI, 56% of China's outbound FDI in 2011was in greenfield projects (such as new plants and business facilities) and 44% involved mergers and acquisitions. In terms of sectors, 51% of China's 2011 FDI went to resources (such as oil and minerals), 22% to chemicals, 14% to services, 12% to industry, and 1% to automotive. SOEs accounted for 72% of Chinese FDI that involved mergers and acquisitions in 2011.[27] A Capital Dragon Index estimates that China's first quarter 2012 outbound FDI was $21.4 billion and that SOEs accounted for 98% of mergers and acquisitions, which were largely in resources.[28]

Figure 10. China's Annual FDI Outflows: 2002-2011

($ billions)

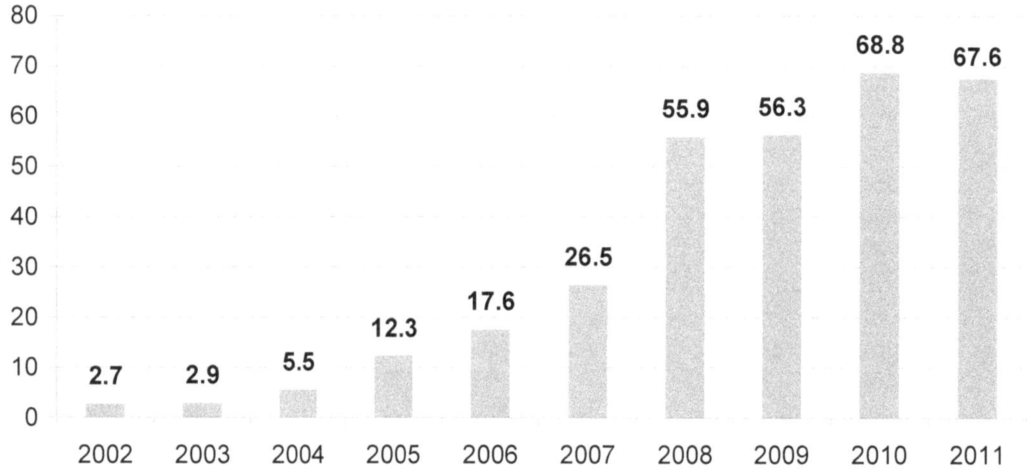

Source: Ministry of Commerce, 2011 Statistical Bulletin of China's Outward Foreign Direct Investment, 2011. Data for 2011 are from the United Nations.

---

[27] A Capital Dragon Index, *2011 Full Year*, available at http://www.acapital hk/dragonindex/datasheets.

[28] A Capital Dragon Index, *2012 Q1*, available at http://www.acapital.hk/dragonindex/datasheets.

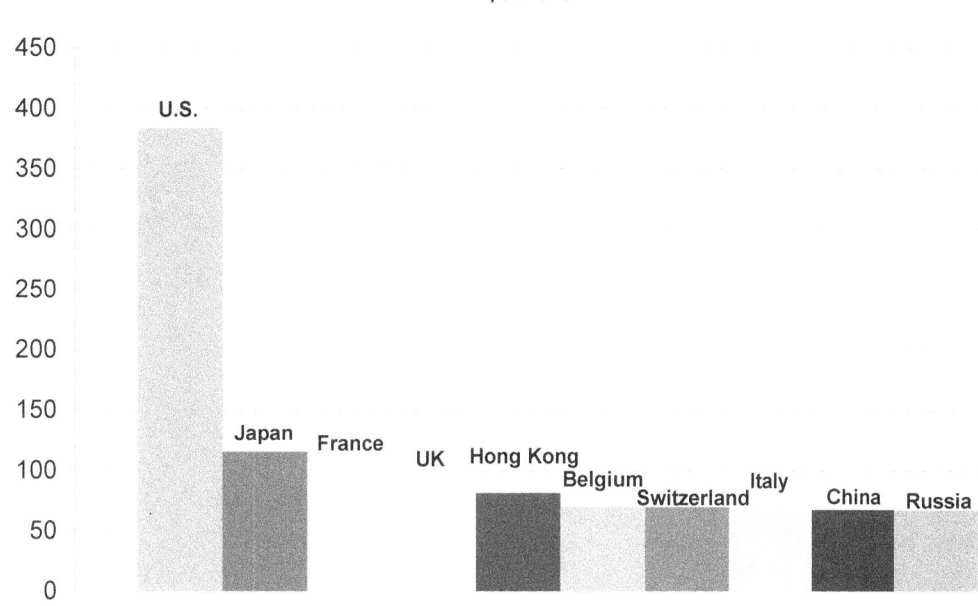

Figure 11. Major Sources of Global FDI Outflows in 2011

$billions

Source: United Nations estimates.

China's Merchandise Trade Patterns

Economic reforms and trade and investment liberalization have helped transform China into a major trading power. Chinese merchandise exports rose from $14 billion in 1979 to $1.9 trillion in 2011, while merchandise imports over this period grew from $16 billion to $1.7 trillion (see **Table 4** and **Figure 12**). From 1990 to 2011, the annual growth of China's exports and imports averaged 19.5% and 18.4%, respectively (see **Figure 13**).

Although Chinese exports and imports dropped sharply in 2009 (over 2008 levels) because of the global economic slowdown, they both recovered in 2010 and exceeded pre-crisis levels. In 2011, China's exports and imports rose by 20.3% and 24.9%, respectively. However, from January-May 2012, China's exports and imports grew by only 8.7% and 6.6%, respectively, over the same period in 2011. China's merchandise trade surplus grew sharply from 2004 to 2008, but fell sharply in 2009-2011. China's merchandise trade surplus fell from its peak of $297.4 billion in 2007 to $157.9 billion – a 46.9% decline. Based on January-May 2012 trade data, China's trade surplus for the full year could fall to about $90 billion.

China overtook Germany in 2009 to become the world's largest merchandise exporter and the second largest importer (see **Figure 14** and **Figure 15**). As indicated in **Figure 16**, China's share of global exports increased from 3.3% in 2000 to 10.4% in 2011; the World Bank projects this figure could increase to 20% by 2030.[29] Merchandise trade surpluses, large-scale foreign

---

[29] The World Bank, China 2030, *Building a Modern, Harmonious, and Creative High-Income Society*, 2012, p. 14. Hereafter referred to as World Bank, China 2030.

investment, and large purchases of foreign currencies to maintain its exchange rate with the dollar and other currencies have enabled China to become by far the world's largest holder foreign exchange reserves at $3.2 trillion at the end of 2011.

Table 4. China's Merchandise World Trade: 1979-2011

($ billions)

Year	Exports	Imports	Trade Balance
1979	13.7	15.7	−2.0
1980	18.1	19.5	−1.4
1985	27.3	42.5	−15.3
1990	62.9	53.9	9.0
1995	148.8	132.1	16.7
2000	249.2	225.1	24.1
2001	266.2	243.6	22.6
2002	325.6	295.2	30.4
2003	438.4	412.8	25.6
2004	593.4	561.4	32.0
2005	762.0	660.1	101.9
2006	969.1	791.5	177.6
2007	1,218.0	955.8	262.2
2008	1,428.9	1,131.5	297.4
2009	1,202.0	1,003.9	198.2
2010	1,578.4	1,393.9	184.5
2011	1,899.3	1,741.4	157.9

Source: *Global Trade Atlas.*

Figure 12. China's Merchandise Trade: 2000-2011

($ billions)

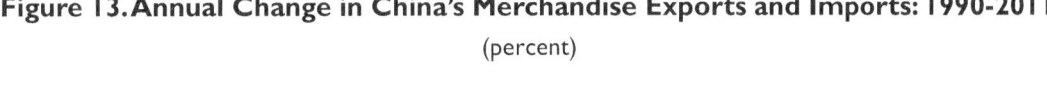

Source: Economist Intelligence Unit.

Figure 13. Annual Change in China's Merchandise Exports and Imports: 1990-2011

(percent)

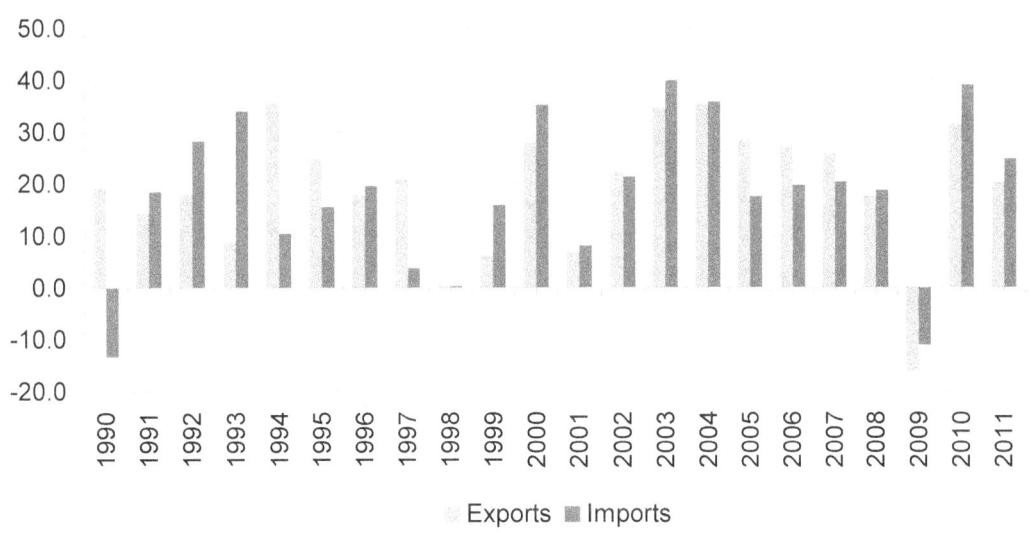

Source: Global Trade Atlas using official Chinese data.

Figure 14. Merchandise Exports by China, Germany and the United States: 1990-2011

($ billions)

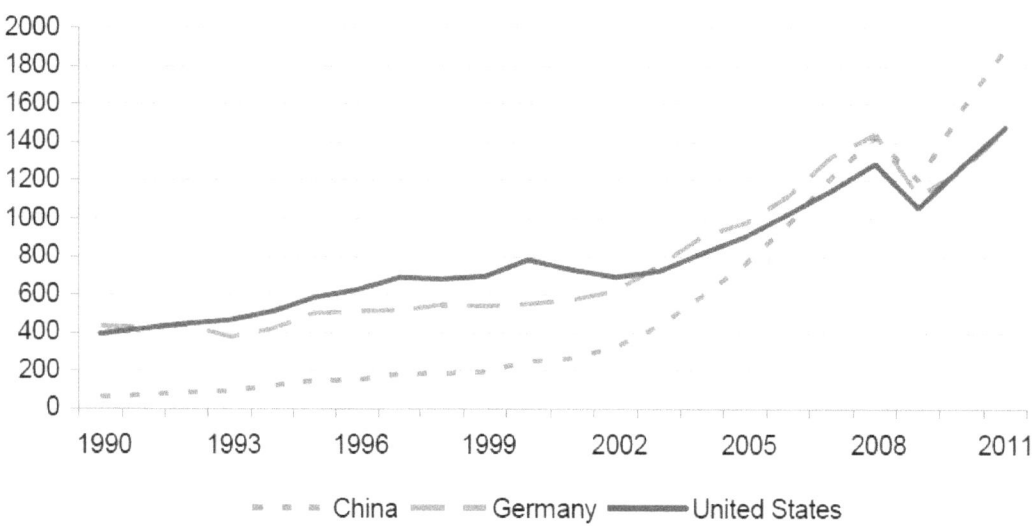

Source: Economist Intelligence Unit.

Note: Top three global importers in 2011.

Figure 15. Merchandise Imports by China, Germany, and the United States: 1990-2011

($ billions)

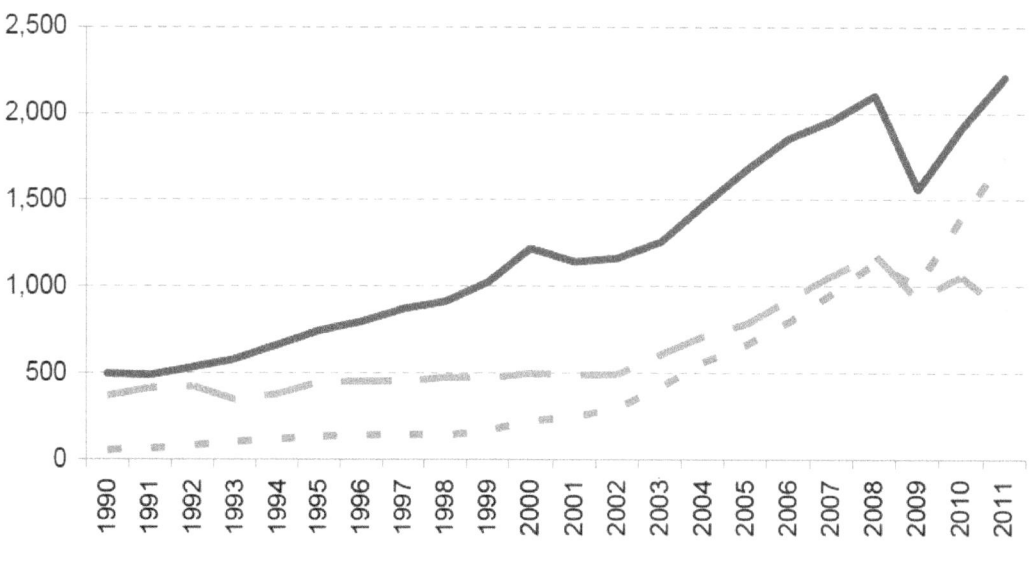

Source: Economist Intelligence Unit.

Note: Top three global importers in 2011.

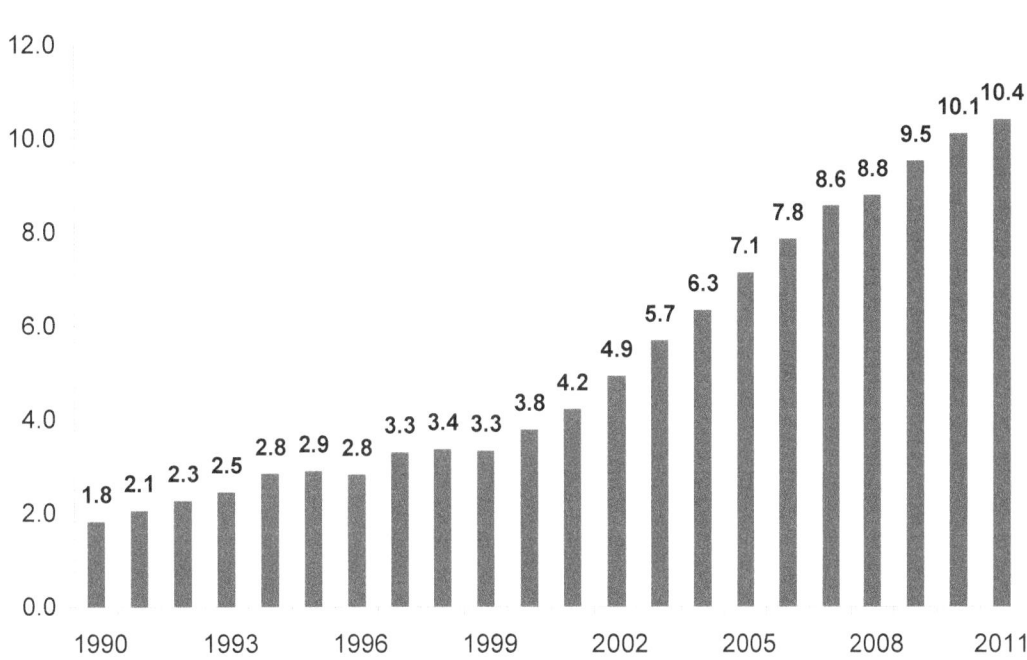

Figure 16. China's Global Share of Merchandise Exports: 1990-2011
($ billions)

Source: Economist Intelligence Unit.

China's Major Trading Partners

Table 5 lists Chinese trade data on its major trading partners in 2011, which included the 27 countries that make up the European Union (EU27), the United States, Japan, and the 10 nations that constitute the Association of Southeast Asian Nations (ASEAN).[30] China's largest export markets were the EU27, the United States, Hong Kong, and ASEAN, while its top sources for imports were the EU27, Japan, ASEAN, and South Korea. According to Chinese data, it maintained substantial trade surpluses with the United States, the EU27, and Hong Kong, but reported large deficits with Taiwan, South Korea, and Japan. China reported that it had a $206.2 billion trade surplus with the United States, but U.S. data show that it had a $295.5 billion deficit with China. These trade imbalance data disparities occur with many of China's other major trading partners as well. China reported that it had a $46.7 billion trade deficit with Japan, while Japan reported that it had a $22.1 billion trade deficit with China. These differences appear to be largely caused by how China's trade via Hong Kong is counted in official trade data. China treats a large share of its exports through Hong Kong as Chinese exports to Hong Kong for statistical

---

[30] ASEAN members include Brunei, Cambodia, Indonesia, Laos, Malaysia, Myanmar (Burma), the Philippines, Singapore, Thailand, and Vietnam.

purposes, while many countries that import Chinese products through Hong Kong generally attribute their origin to China for statistical purposes, including the United States.[31]

Table 5. China's Major Trading Partners in 2011

($ billions)

Country	Total Trade	Chinese Exports	Chinese Imports	China's Trade Balance	Foreign Partner's Reported Trade Balance with China
European Union	567.2	356.0	211.2	144.8	-217.6
United States	442.4	324.3	118.1	206.2	-295.5
Japan	342.1	147.7	194.4	-46.7	-22.1
ASEAN	362.4	169.9	192.5	-22.6	NA
Hong Kong	277.9	267.5	10.4	257.1	26.6
South Korea	250.6	82.9	167.7	-84.8	47.8
Taiwan	155.0	30.1	124.9	-94.8	34.7
Total Chinese Trade	**3,640.7**	**1,899.3**	**1,741.4**	**157.9**	--

Source: Global Trade Atlas and World Trade Atlas.

Note: Rankings according to China's total trade in 2011.

Major Chinese Trade Commodities

China's abundance of low-cost labor has made it internationally competitive in many low-cost, labor-intensive manufactures. The average hourly labor cost for manufacturing in China in 2010 (at $2) was 5.7% the cost in the United States (at $35).[32] As a result, manufactured products constitute a significant share of China's trade. A substantial amount of China's imports is comprised of parts and components that are assembled into finished products, such as consumer electronic products and computers, and then exported. Often, the value-added to such products in China by Chinese workers is relatively small compared to the total value of the product when it is shipped abroad.

China's top 10 exports and imports in 2011 are listed in **Table 6** and **Table 7**, respectively, using the harmonized tariff system (HTS) on a two-digit level. Major exports included electrical machinery (such as computers and parts), machinery, knit apparel, and woven apparel, while major imports included electrical machinery, mineral fuel, machinery, and ores.

---

[31] See CRS Report RS22640, *What's the Difference?—Comparing U.S. and Chinese Trade Data*, by Michael F. Martin.

[32] In addition, the overall average monthly wage in China, at $539 (nominal U.S. dollars) in 2011, was about 13% U.S. levels (although the disparity would lessen if purchasing power data were used). Source: Economist Intelligence Unit data tool.

Table 6. Major Chinese Exports: 2011

HS Code	Description	$billions	Percent of Total	2011/2010 % Change
	World	1,899.3	100	20.3
85	Electrical machinery (such as computers and parts)	445.8	23.5	14.6
84	Machinery	353.9	18.6	14.2
61	Knit apparel	80.2	4.2	20.2
62	Woven apparel	63.1	3.3	16.0
90	Optical, photographic, cinematographic, measuring checking, precision, medical or surgical instruments and apparatus; parts and accessories thereof	60.7	3.2	16.5
94	Furniture and bedding	59.4	3.1	17.3
73	Iron and steel products	51.2	2.7	30.8
87	Vehicles, except railway (mainly auto parts, motorcycles, trucks, and bicycles)	49.6	2.6	29.2
39	Plastic	45.5	2.4	30.9
89	Ships and boats	43.7	2.3	8.5

Source: *World Trade Atlas*, using official Chinese statistics.

Notes: Top 10 exports in 2011, 2-digit level, harmonized tariff system.

Table 7. Major Chinese Imports: 2011

HS Code	Description	$ billions	Percent of Total	2011/2010 % change
	World	1,741.4	100	24.9
85	Electrical machinery	351.0	20.2	11.6
27	Mineral fuel, oil etc.	273.5	15.7	45.2
84	Machinery	199.6	11.5	15.8
26	Ores, slag, and ash	150.7	8.7	39.5
90	Optical, photographic, cinematographic, measuring, checking, precision, medical or surgical instruments and apparatus; parts and accessories thereof	99.0	5.7	10.4
39	Plastic	70.2	4.0	10.2
87	Vehicles, not railway (mainly autos and parts)	65.3	3.8	32.2
29	Organic chemicals	63.2	3.6	31.0
74	Copper and articles thereof	54.3	3.1	18.0
98	Special Classification	49.5	2.8	168.5

Source: *World Trade Atlas*, using official Chinese statistics.

Notes: Top 10 imports in 2011, two-digit level, harmonized tariff schedule.

China's Growing Appetite for Energy

China's rapid economic growth has fueled a growing demand for energy, such as petroleum and coal, and that demand is becoming an increasingly important factor in determining global energy prices. According to the International Energy Agency (IEA), China overtook the United States in 2009 as the world's largest energy user (in comparison, China's energy use was only half that of that of the United States in 2000). According to IEA projections, China's demand for energy from 2008 (the baseline year) to 2035 will account for 30% of the projected increase in global demand for energy during this period. By 2035, China is projected to consume 70% more energy than the United States (even though, on a per capita basis, China's energy consumption will be less than half of U.S. levels).[33]

China is the world's second largest consumer of oil products (after the United States) at 9.8 million barrels per day (bpd) in 2011 (compared to 3.9 million in 1997), and that level rises to 16.9 million bpd by 2035.[34] China became a net oil importer (i.e., imports minus exports) in 1993. Net oil imports grew from 632 thousand bpd in 1997 to about 5.0 million bpd in 2010 (see **Figure 17**), making it the world's second largest net oil importer after the United States.[35] China's net oil imports are projected to rise to 13.1 million bpd by 2030, a level that would be comparable to the European Union in that year.[36]

---

[33] International Energy Agency, *2011 World Energy Outlook*, November 2011, available at http://www.iea.org/weo.

[34] U.S. Energy Information Administration, *Forecasts and Analysis*, at http://www.eia.doe.gov/oiaf/forecasting.html.

[35] China overtook Japan as the second largest net oil importer in 2009.

[36] EIA, *International Energy Outlook*, September 19, 2011, available at http://www.eia.gov/forecasts/ieo.

Figure 17. China's Net Oil Imports: 1997-2011

(Thousands BPD)

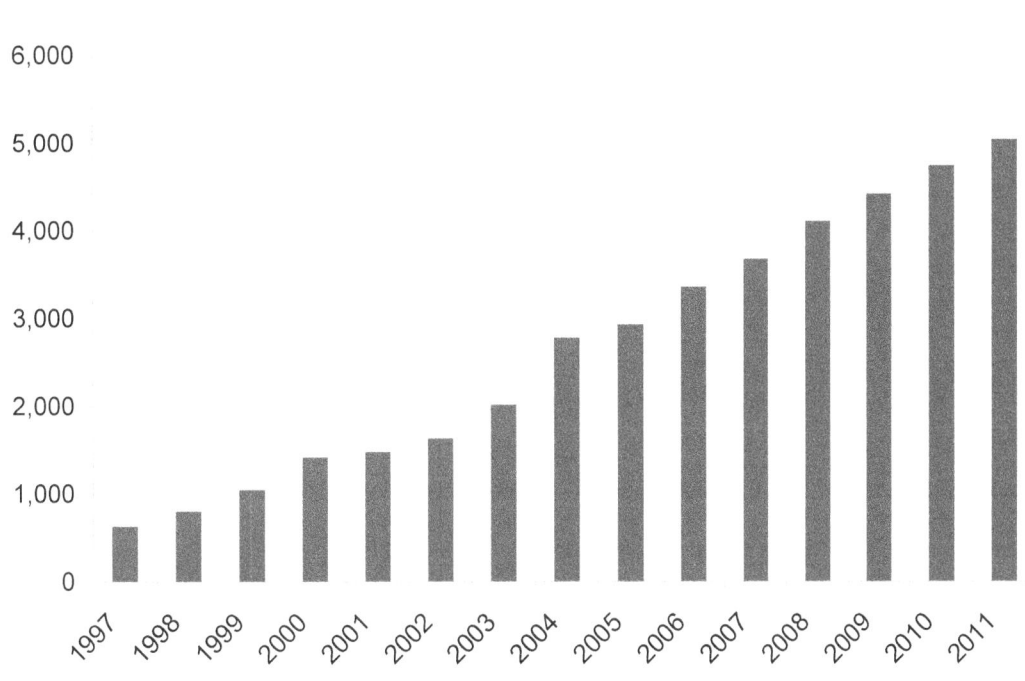

Source: U.S. Energy Administration, China Energy Newswire, and British Petroleum June 2010 Statistical Review of World Energy. Data for 2010 and 2011 from China Daily.

China's Regional and Bilateral Free Trade Agreements

The Chinese government has maintained an active policy of boosting trade and investment ties around the world, especially with countries in Asia. To that end, China has entered into a number of regional and bilateral trade agreements, or is in the process of doing so. China currently has free trade agreements (FTAs) with ASEAN, Pakistan, Chile, Hong Kong, Macau, New Zealand, Singapore, Pakistan, Peru, and Costa Rica. China also has an economic cooperation framework agreement (ECFA) with Taiwan. China is currently in the process of negotiating FTAs with the Cooperation Council for the Arab States of the Gulf (which includes Saudi Arabia, Kuwait, the United Arab Emirates, Qatar, and Bahrain), Australia, Iceland, Norway, Switzerland, and the Southern African Customs Union (which includes Botswana, Lesotho, Namibia, and Swaziland). In May 2012, China, Japan, and South Korea agreed to begin negotiations for an FTA in 2012. China has also considered negotiating an FTA with India, but with little progress to date.[37]

---

[37] Chinese Ministry of Commerce, *China FTA Network*, available at http://fta.mofcom.gov.cn/english/fta_qianshu.shtml.

Major Long-Term Challenges Facing the Chinese Economy

China's economy has shown remarkable growth over the past several years, and many economists project that it will enjoy fairly healthy growth in the near future. However, economists caution that these projections are likely to occur only if China continues to make major reforms to its economy. Failure to implement such reforms could endanger future growth. They note that China's current economic model has resulted in a number of negative economic (and social) outcomes, such as over-reliance on fixed investment and exporting for its economic growth, extensive inefficiencies that exist in many sectors (due largely to government industrial policies), wide-spread pollution, and growing income inequality, to name a few. Many of China's economic problems and challenges stem from its incomplete transition to a free market economy and from imbalances that have resulted from the government's goal of economic growth at all costs.

China's Incomplete Transition to a Market Economy

Despite China's three-decade history of widespread economic reforms, Chinese officials contend that China is a "socialist-market economy." This appears to indicate that the government accepts and allows the use of free market forces in a number of areas to help grow the economy, but where the government still plays a major role in the country's economic development.

Industrial Policies and SOEs

According to the World Bank, "China has become one of the world's most active users of industrial policies and administrations."[38] According to one estimate, China's SOEs may account for up of 50% of non-agriculture GDP.[39] In addition, although the number of SOEs has declined sharply, they continue to dominate a number of sectors (such as petroleum and mining, telecommunications, utilities, transportation, and various industrial sectors); are shielded from competition; are the main sectors encouraged to invest overseas; and dominate the listings on China's stock indexes.[40] One study found that SOEs constituted 50% of the 500 largest manufacturing companies in China and 61% of the top 500 service sector enterprises.[41] It is estimated that there were 154,000 SOEs as of 2008, and while these accounted for only 3.1% of all enterprises in China, they held 30% of the value of corporate assets in the manufacturing and services sectors.[42] Of the 58 Chinese firms on the 2011 *Fortune* Global 500 list, 54 were

---

[38] The World Bank, *China:2030,* p. 114.

[39] U.S.-China Economic and Security Review Commission, An Analysis of State-owned Enterprises and State Capitalism in China, by Andrew Szamosszegi and Cole Kyle, October 26, 2011, p.1.

[40] The nature of China's SOEs has become increasing complex. Many SOEs appear to be run like private companies. For example, and a number of SOEs have made initial public offerings in China's stock markets and those in other countries (including the United States), although the Chinese government is usually the largest shareholder. It is not clear to what extent the Chinese government attempts to influence decisions made by the SOE's which have become shareholding companies.

[41] Xiao Geng, Xiuke Yang, and Anna Janus, *State-owned Enterprises in China, Reform Dynamics and Impacts*, 2009, p.155.

[42] The World Bank, *State-Owned Enterprises in China: How Big Are They?*, January 19, 2010.

identified as having government ownership of 50% or more. [43] The World Bank estimates that more than one in four SOEs lose money. [44]

The Banking System

China's banking system is largely controlled by the central government, which attempts to ensure that capital (credit) flows to industries deemed by the government to be essential to China's economic development. SOEs, which are believed to receive preferential credit treatment by government banks, while private firms must often pay higher interest rates or obtain credit elsewhere. According to one estimate, SOEs accounted for 85% ($1.4 trillion) of all bank loans in 2009. [45] In addition, the government sets interest rates for depositors at very low rates, often below the rate of inflation, which keeps the price of capital relatively low for firms. [46] It is believed that oftentimes SOEs do not repay their loans, which may have saddled the banks with a large amount of non-performing loans. In addition, local governments are believed to have borrowed extensively from state banks shortly after the global economic slowdown began to impact the Chinese economy to fund infrastructure and other initiatives. Some contend these measures could further add to the amount of non-performing loans held by the banks. Many analysts contend that one of the biggest weaknesses of the banking system is that it lacks the ability to ration and allocate credit according to market principles, such as risk assessment.

An Undervalued Currency

China does not allow its currency to float and therefore must make large-scale purchases of dollars to keep the exchange rate within certain target levels. Although the renminbi (RMB) has appreciated against the dollar in real terms by about 40% since reforms were introduced in July 2005, analysts contend that it remains highly undervalued. [47] China's undervalued currency makes its exports less expensive, and its imports more expensive, than would occur under a floating exchange rate system. In order to maintain its exchange rate target, the government must purchases foreign currency (such as the dollar) by expanding the money supply. This makes it much more difficult for the government to use monetary policy to combat inflation. [48]

Many economists argue that China's industrial policies have sharply limited competition and the growth of the private sector, caused over-capacity in many industries, and distorted markets by

---

[43] Global 500, The World's Largest Corporations," *Fortune*, July 25, 2011, available at http://money.cnn.com/magazines/fortune/global500/2011/index html.

[44] World Bank, *China 2030*, p.25.

[45] The Economist, *State Capitalism's Global Reach, New Masters of the Universe, How State Enterprise is Spreading*, January 21, 2012, available at http://www.economist.com/node/21542925.

[46] Some economists argue that a significant portion of China's SOEs could not stay in business if they had to pay a market-based interest rate for credit.

[47] See CRS Report RS21625, *China's Currency Policy: An Analysis of the Economic Issues*, by Wayne M. Morrison and Marc Labonte.

[48] If Chinese banks raised interest rates in an effort to control inflation, overseas investors might to try to shift funds to China (through illegal means) to take advantage of the higher Chinese rates. The Chinese government has had difficulty blocking such inflows of "hot money." Such inflows force the government to boost the money supply to buy up the foreign currency necessary to maintain the targeted peg. Expanding the money supply contributes to easy credit policies by the banks, which has contributed to overcapacity in a number of sectors, such as steel, and speculative asset bubbles (such as in real estate). This often forces the government to use administrative controls to limit credit to certain sectors.

artificially lowering the costs of various factor costs (such as capital, water, land, and energy) below market levels in order to promote targeted industrial sectors. Such policies have come at the expense of other (non-industrial) sectors of the economy, such as services.

Implications of China's "Unbalanced" Economic Growth Model

China's economic model, until recently, has emphasized rapid economic growth above nearly all other considerations. Various data show that, while China's GDP has risen rapidly over past 33 years, Chinese households do not appear to have shared equally in that growth. In addition, China's economic model has resulted in a number of significant problems that may negatively affect future growth.

Overdependence on Exporting and Fixed Investment

The International Monetary Fund (IMF) estimates that that fixed investment related to tradable goods plus net exports together accounted for over 60% of China's GDP growth from 2001 to 2008 (up from 40% from 1990 to 2000), which was significantly higher than in the G-7 countries (16%), the euro area (30%) and the rest of Asia (35%). China's fixed investment as a percentage of GDP is the highest of any major economy and its importance has been growing. As shown in **Figure 18**, fixed investment as a percent of GDP increased from 25% in 1990 to 48.5% in 2011. On the other hand, during the same period, private consumption of as a percent of GDP fell from 48.8% to 33.9%.[49] China's private consumption as a share of GDP is the lowest of any major economy.[50] In addition, as indicated in **Figure 19**, personal disposable income in China as a share of GDP has also been falling over the past decade or so, from 47.6% in 2000 to 42.2% in 2011.[51] China's overall savings rate as a percent of GDP in 2011 was 52.1%, which was the highest rate of any major economy.

Many economists contend that the falling share of private consumption and disposable income relative to GDP is largely caused by two main factors: China's banking policies and the lack of an adequate social safety net. The Chinese government places restrictions on the export of capital. As a result, Chinese households put a large share of their savings in domestic banks. The Chinese government sets the interest rate on deposits. Often this rate is below the rate of inflation, which lowers household income. Some economists consider this policy to constitute a transfer of wealth from Chinese households to Chinese firms which benefit from low interest rates. This "tax" on household income negatively affects household consumption. Secondly, China's lack of an adequate social safety net (such as pensions, health care, unemployment insurance, and education) induces households to save a large portion of their income. According to one estimate, the average saving rate of urban households relative to their disposable incomes rose from 18% in 1995 to nearly 29% in 2009.[52] Corporations are also a major contributor the high savings rate in China. Many Chinese firms, especially SOEs, do not pay out dividends and thus are able to retain

---

[49] Private consumption in China has been rising rapidly over the past several years, but not as fast as over parts of the economy.

[50] In comparison, the U.S. figure was 71.1%.

[51] That rate was 43.4% in 1990.

[52] VOX, *The Puzzle of China's Rising Household Saving Rate*, by Marcos Chamon, Kai Liu, and Eswar Prasad, January 18, 2011, available at http://voxeu.org/index.php?q=node/6028.

most of their earnings. Many economists contend that requiring the SOEs to pay dividends could boost private consumption in China.

Figure 18. Chinese Gross Savings, Gross Fixed Investment, and Private Consumption as a Percent of GDP: 1990-2011

(percent)

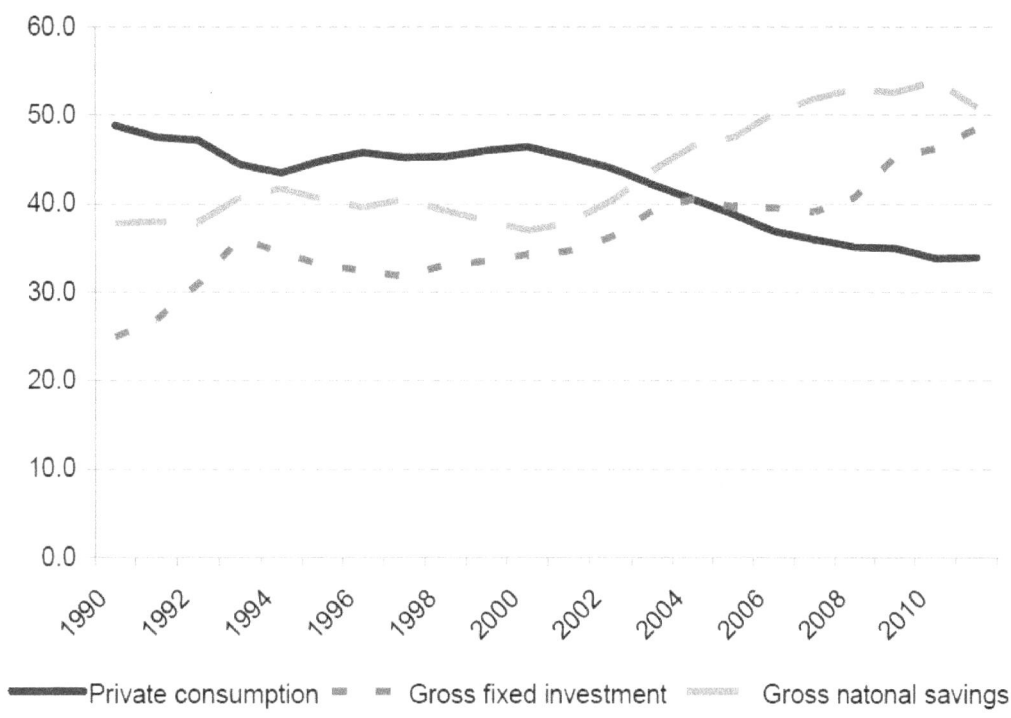

Source: Economist Intelligence Unit.

Figure 19. Chinese Disposable Personal Income as a Percent of GDP: 2000-2011

(percent)

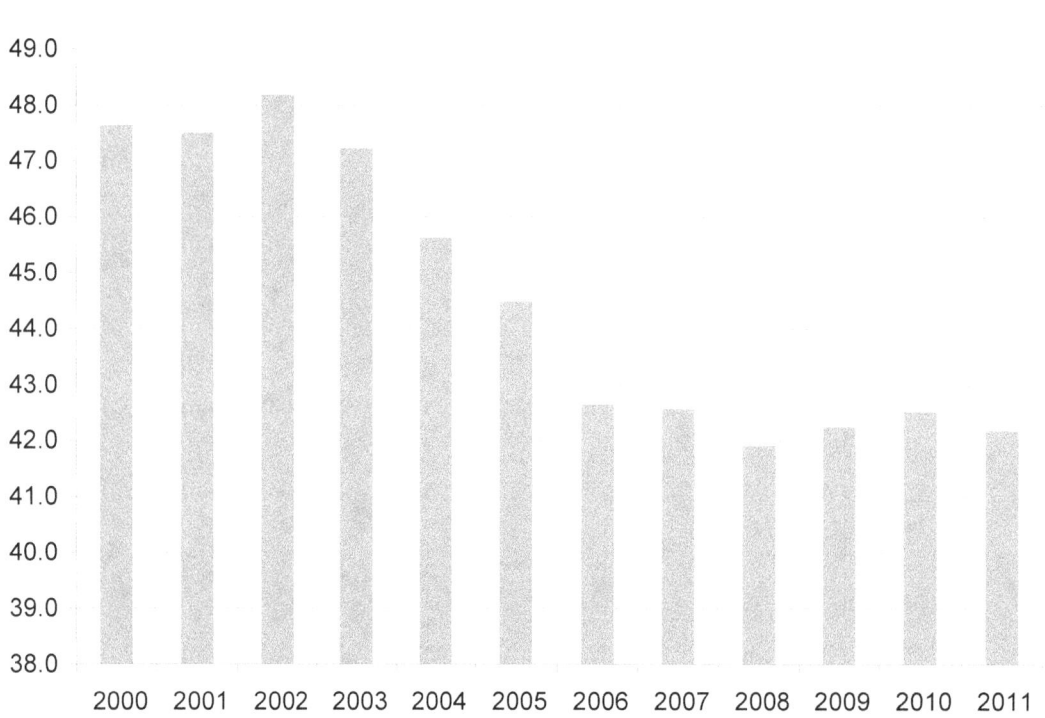

Source: Economist Intelligence Unit.

Growing Pollution

China's economic growth model has emphasized the growth of heavy industry in China, much of which is energy-intensive and high polluting. The level of pollution in China continues to worsen, posing series health risks to the population. The Chinese government often disregards its own environmental laws in order to promote rapid economic growth. According to the World Bank, 20 out of 30 of the world's most polluted cities are in China, with significant costs to the economy (such as health problems, crop failures and water shortages). According to one government official estimate in 2006, environmental damage costs the country $226 billion, or 10% of the country's GDP, each year.[53] The Chinese government estimated that in 2004 there were over 300 million people living in rural areas that drank unsafe water (caused by chemicals and other contaminants).Toxic spills in 2005 and 2006 threatened the water supply of millions of people. China is the largest producer and consumer of coal, which accounts for about 70% of China's energy use. In October 2009, China's media reported that thousands of children living near smelters had been found to have excessive amounts of lead in their blood. Although growing environmental degradation has been recognized as a serious problem by China's central government, it has found it difficult to induce local governments to comply with environmental laws, especially when such officials feel doing so will come at the expense of economic growth.

---

[53] China Daily, June 6, 2006.

The EIA projects that by 2035, China's carbon dioxide emissions could be nearly double its current levels.[54] A study by ExxonMobil, by 2030, China's CO2 emissions could equal the combined level in the United States and EU combined.[55]

Other Challenges

China's economy faces a number of social and political challenges as well:

- **Public unrest.** For China's Communist Party leadership, a growing economy is its main source of political legitimacy. However, every year numerous protests occur in China over a number of issues, including pollution, government corruption, and land seizures. A number of protests in China have stemmed in part from frustrations among many Chinese (especially peasants) that they are not benefitting from China's economic reforms and rapid growth, and perceptions that those who are getting rich are doing so because they have connections with government officials. A 2005 United Nations report stated that the income gap between the urban and rural areas was among the highest in the world and warned that this gap threatens social stability. The report urged China to take greater steps to improve conditions for the rural poor, and bolster education, health care, and the social safety net.[56] It is estimated that 300 million people in China (mainly in rural areas) lacked health insurance, and many that do have basic insurance must pay a significant amount of medical expenses out of their own pocket.[57]

- **The lack of the rule of law** in China has led to widespread government corruption, financial speculation, and misallocation of investment funds. In many cases, government "connections," not market forces, are the main determinant of successful firms in China. Many U.S. firms find it difficult to do business in China because rules and regulations are generally not consistent or transparent, contracts are not easily enforced, and intellectual property rights are not protected (due to the lack of an independent judicial system). The relative lack of the rule of law and widespread government corruption in China limit competition and undermine the efficient allocation of goods and services in the economy.

- **Poor government regulatory environment**. China maintains a weak and relatively decentralized government structure to regulate economic activity in China. Laws and regulations often go unenforced or are ignored by local government officials. As a result, many firms cut corners in order to maximize profits. This has lead to a proliferation of unsafe food and consumer products being sold in China or exported abroad. Lack of government enforcement of food safety laws led to a massive recall of melamine-tainted infant milk formula that reportedly killed at least four children and sickened 53,000 others in 2008.

---

[54] EIA, International Energy Outlook, September 19, 2011, available at http://www.eia.gov/forecasts/ieo.

[55] ExxonMobil, *The Outlook for Energy*, A View to 2030, December 29, 2009, p. 4.

[56] *China's Human Development Report 2005*.

[57] Washington Post, October 29, 2009.

Plans Announced by the Chinese Government to Reform and Restructure the Economy

Various government officials have publicly stated the need for China to change course from its traditional economic growth model of growth at all cost to one that balances economic growth with a number of social goals in order to develop a "socialist harmonious society," and to further modernize the economy. In March 2007, Chinese Premier Wen Jiabao stated that there are "structural problems in China's economy which cause unsteady, unbalanced, uncoordinated and unsustainable development." He defined "unsteady development" as overheated investment, excessive credit and liquidity, and merchandise trade and current account surpluses. "Unbalanced development" was described as economic disparities between rural and urban areas, regions of the country, and between economic and social development. "Uncoordinated development" was described as the lack of balance between various sectors of the economy (especially in regards to the services sector) and between investment and consumption (i.e., economic growth is mainly driven by investment and exports rather than consumer demand). Lastly, "unsustainable development" referred to problems caused by China's inefficient use of energy and resources and failure to protect the environment.

The Central Government Five-Year Plans

China's last two five-year plans (FYP), the 11th FYP (2006-2010) and the 12th FYP (2011-2015), have placed strong emphasis on promoting consumer demand, addressing income disparities (such as by boosting spending on social safety net programs) boosting energy efficiency, reducing pollution, improving the rule of law, and deepening economic reforms. Those plans have also identified a number of industries and technologies that the government has targeted for development (see text box).

China's 12th Five-Year Plan[58]

China's Five-Year Plans (FYPs), which have been issued by the government since 1953. The FYP is the major vehicle for the government to establish broad economic and social goals for the time period under consideration, to coordinate investments between the central and local governments, and to oversee implementation of policy. Not only does the plan influence investments by government entities, it also provides direction for bank lending and government approvals and regulation of private and semi-private industries. In March 2011, China's National People's Congress approved the 12th Five-Year Plan (covering the years 2011 to 2015).

The 12th FYP (2011-2015) contains three broad themes or areas of focus: (1) economic restructuring, (2) promoting greater social equality, and (3) protecting the environment. Chinese industrial policy comes into play primarily in economic restructuring but also is apparent in the other areas of focus. Particularly noteworthy is the targeting of seven strategic emerging industries that are intended to become the backbone of China's economy in the future and to be able to compete well on a global scale. These seven industries are: (1) biotechnology, (2) new energy, (3) high-end equipment manufacturing, (4) energy conservation and environmental protection, (5) clean-energy vehicles, (6) new materials, and (7) next-generation information technology. The government reportedly intends to spend up to $2.1 trillion on these industries during the 12th FYP. Some of the highlights of the FYP include:

- achieving an average real GDP growth rate of 7% and ensuring that incomes rise at least as fast as GDP;

- consolidating inefficient sectors and promoting the services industry (with the goal of expanding service sector output to account for 47% of GDP—up four percentage points from the current level);

- promoting energy saving and new energy industries, promoting the development of nuclear, water, wind, and solar power, and expanding non-fossil fuel to account for 11.4% of primary energy consumption;

- welcoming foreign investment in modern agriculture, high-technology, and environmental protection industries;

- turning coastal regions from "world's factory" to hubs of research and development, high-end manufacturing, and services;

- lengthening high-speed railway and highway networks;

- increasing expenditure on R&D to account for 2.2 percent GDP;

- expanding non-fossil fuel to account for 11.4% of primary energy consumption;

- cutting water consumption per unit of value-added industrial output by 30%, energy consumption per unit of GDP by 16%, and carbon dioxide emission per unit of GDP by 17%;

- transfer the coastal regions from the "world's factory" to hubs of R&D, high-end manufacturing, and environmental protection industries;

- increasing the minimum wage by no less than 13% on average each year; and

- building 36 million affordable apartments for low-income people.

Sources: Xinhua News Agency, *Highlights of China's 12th Five-Year Plan*, March 5, 2011; and APCO Worldwide, *China's 12th Five-Year Plan: How it Actually Works and What's in Store For the Next Five Years*, December 10, 2010.

The Drive for "Indigenous Innovation"

Many of the industrial policies that China has implemented or formulated since 2006 appear to stem largely from a comprehensive document issued by China's State Council (the highest executive organ of state power) in 1996 titled "the National Medium-and Long-Term Program for Science and Technology Development (2006-2020)," often referred to as the MLP. The MLP appears to represent an ambitious plan to modernize the structure of China's economy by transforming it from a global center of low-tech manufacturing to a major center of innovation (by the year 2020) and a global innovation leader by 2050. As some observers describe it, China

---

[58] "Highlights of China's Draft 12th Five-Year Plan," *Xinhua*, March 5, 2011.

wants to go from a model of "made in China" to "innovated in China." It also seeks to sharply reduce the country's dependence on foreign technology. The MLP includes the stated goals of "indigenous innovation, leapfrogging in priority fields, enabling development, and leading the future."[59] Some of the broad goals of the MLP state that by 2020:

- The progress of science and technology will contribute 60% or above to China's development.

- The country's reliance on foreign technology will decline to 30% or below (from an estimated current level of 50%).

- Gross expenditures for research and development (R&D) would rise to 2.5% of gross domestic product (from 1.3% in 2005). Priority areas for increased R&D include space programs, aerospace development and manufacturing, renewable energy, computer science, and life sciences.[60]

The document states that "China must place the strengthening of indigenous innovative capability at the core of economic restructuring, growth model change, and national competitiveness enhancement. Building an innovation-oriented country is therefore a major strategic choice for China's future development." This goal, according to the document, is to be achieved by formulating and implementing regulations in the country's government procurement law to "encourage and protect indigenous innovation," establishing a coordination mechanism for government procurement of indigenous innovative products, requiring a first-buy policy for major domestically made high-tech equipment and products that possess proprietary intellectual property rights, providing policy support to enterprises in procuring domestic high-tech equipment, and developing "relevant technology standards" through government procurement.

Challenges to U.S. Policy of China's Economic Rise

China's rapid economic growth and emergence as major economic power have given China's leadership increased confidence in its economic model. Many believe the key challenges for the United States are to convince China that: (1) it has a stake in maintaining the international trading system, which is largely responsible for its economic rise, and to take a more active leadership role in maintaining that system; and (2) that further economic and trade reforms are the surest way for China to grow and modernize its economy. For example, by boosting domestic spending and allowing its currency to appreciate, China would import more, which would help speed economic recovery in other countries, promote more stable and balanced economic growth in China, and lessen trade protectionist pressures around the world. Lowering trade barriers on imports would boost competition in China, lower costs for consumers, and increase economic efficiency. However, many U.S. stakeholders are concerned that China's efforts to boost the development of indigenous innovation and technology could result in greater intervention by the state (such as subsidies and trade and investment barriers), which could negatively affect U.S. IP-intensive firms. Failure by China to take meaningful steps to rebalance its economy could

---

[59] The MLP identifies main areas and priority topics, including energy, water and mineral resources, the environment, agriculture, manufacturing, communications and transport, information industry and modern service industries, population and health, urbanization and urban development, public security, and national defense. The report also identifies 16 major special projects and 8 "pioneer technologies."

[60] *R&D Magazine*, December 22, 2009.

increase tensions with its trading partners, especially if China's share of global exports continues to increase rapidly, and if that increase is viewed as being the result of non-market policies that give Chinese exports an unfair competitive advantage.[61] Some economist contend that some economic rebalancing by China appears to taken place in recent years, noting that China's current account surplus as a percent of GDP declined from a historical high of 10.1% in 2007 to 2.8% in 2011 (see **Figure 20**). However, ass indicated in **Figure 21**, fixed investment has been the largest contributor to China's economic growth over the past five years, rather than private consumption.

Figure 20. Current Account Balances as a Percent of GDP for China and the United States: 2000-2011

(percent)

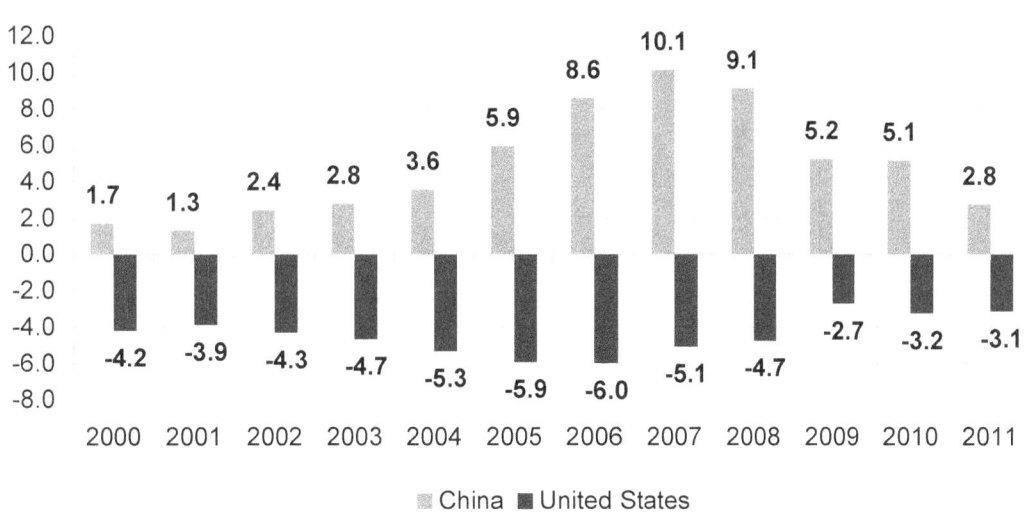

Source: International Monetary Fund.

---

[61] Sharp increases in Chinese exports of higher-end manufacturing could also raise trade tensions between China and its major trading partners. This has already occurred in some areas, such as wind turbines and solar panels.

Figure 21. Sources of China's GDP Growth: 2007-2011

(% points)

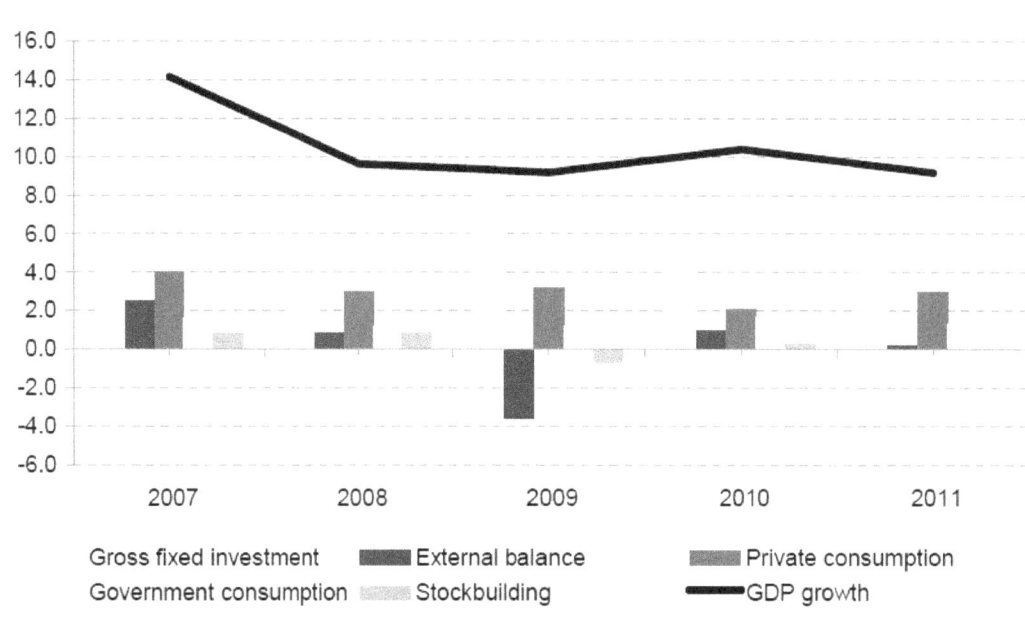

Source: Economist Intelligence Unit.

Opinions differ as to the most effective way of dealing with China on major economic issues. Some support a policy of engagement with China using various forums, such as the U.S.-China Strategic and Economic Dialogue (S&ED), which holds discussions on major long-term economic issues the highest government level. Others support a somewhat mixed policy of using engagement when possible, coupled with a more aggressive use of the World Trade Organization (WTO) dispute settlement procedures to address China's unfair trade policies. Still others, who see China as a growing threat to the U.S. economy and the global trading system, advocate a policy of trying to contain China's economic power and using punitive measures when needed to force China to "play by the rules."

China's growing economic power has made it a critical and influential player on the global stage on a number of issues important to U.S. interests, such as global economic cooperation, climate change, nuclear proliferation, and North Korean aggression.[62] China is in a position to help advance U.S. interests or to frustrate them. China's rising economy has also enabled it to boost its military capabilities, raising the prospects that China could use that power to project its interests globally, which could bring it into conflict with the United States and its allies.

U.S. policymakers face a number of complex challenges on how to deal with these issues. Can the U.S. compel better behavior from China via quiet diplomacy or public confrontation? Has U.S. leverage over Beijing lessened in the wake of China's economic rise, and has China's leverage over Washington increased?

---

[62] For additional information on these issues, see CRS Report R41108, *U.S.-China Relations: Policy Issues*, by Susan V. Lawrence and Thomas Lum.

Author Contact Information

Wayne M. Morrison
Specialist in Asian Trade and Finance
wmorrison@crs.loc.gov, 7-7767